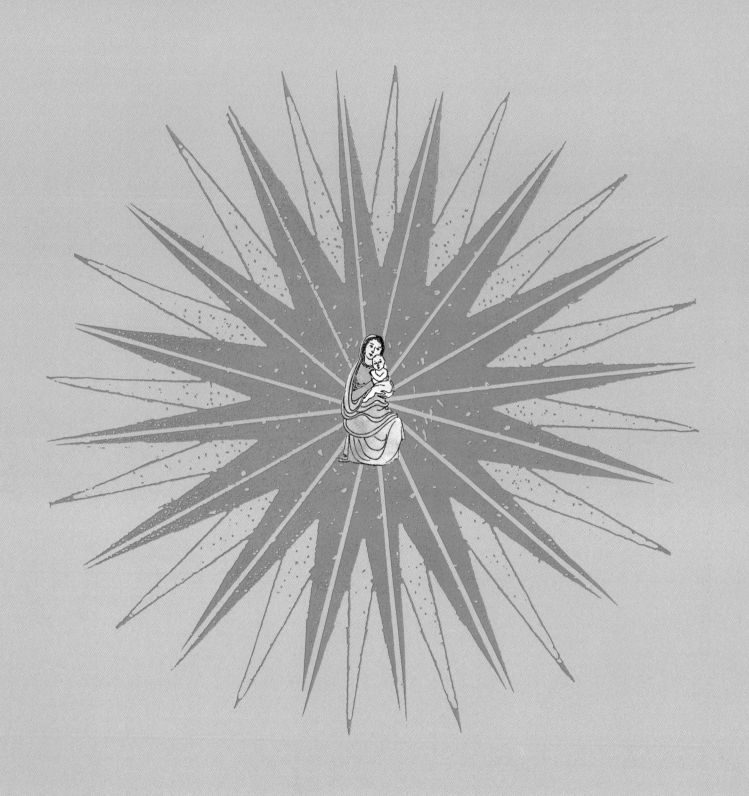

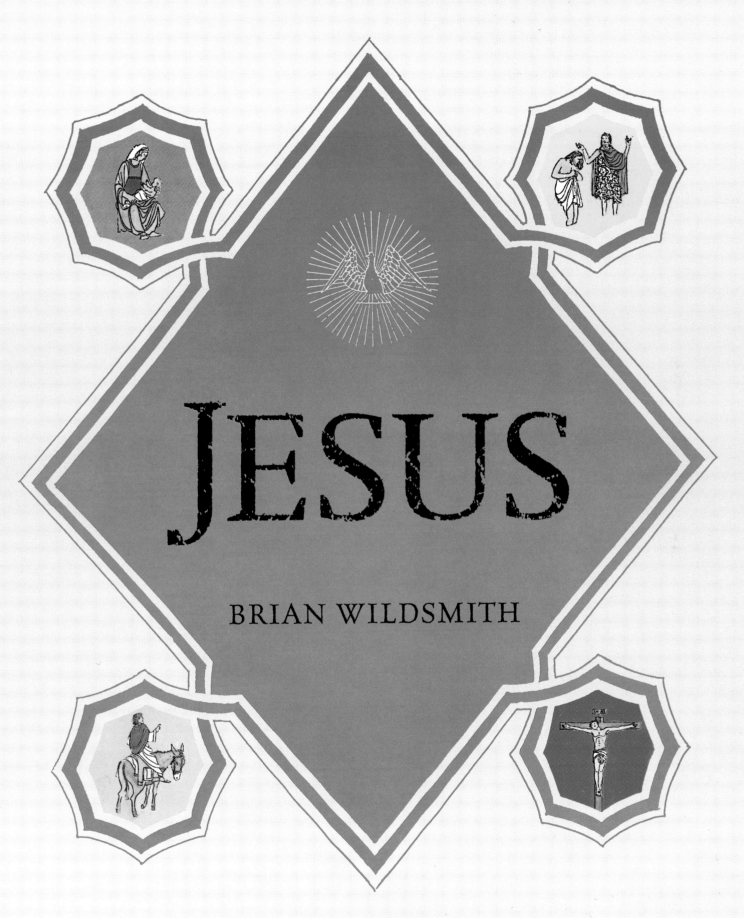

JESUS

BRIAN WILDSMITH

OXFORD

UNIVERSITY PRESS

The angel Gabriel was sent by God to a young girl called Mary who lived in Nazareth.
'God has chosen you,' said the angel. 'You will have a son and you will give him the name
Jesus. He will be called the Son of God.'

Almost nine months later, Mary and her husband Joseph had to make a long journey to
Bethlehem.

They had to sleep in a stable because there was no room for them in the inn.
    And there, surrounded by animals, Mary's son was born under the light of a shining star.

Shepherds were guarding their sheep when angels appeared in the sky. They told them the good news that the Son of God had been born in Bethlehem.

The shepherds hurried to Bethlehem and found Mary and Joseph, and the baby Jesus lying in a manger.

Meanwhile three wise men from the East came to see King Herod. 'Where is the new-born King of the Jews?' they asked. 'We have seen his star rising.'

The chief priests replied, 'The prophets say he will be born in Bethlehem.'

Then Herod told the wise men: 'Go and find the child. And when you have found him, come back and tell me.'

The wise men travelled on, following the star, until it stopped above the stable where the little child had been born. They went in and opened their treasure chests and gave him presents of gold, frankincense, and myrrh.

That night an angel appeared to Joseph and said, 'Take Mary and the baby to Egypt. Herod's soldiers are looking for Jesus. They want to kill him.' So Joseph got up at once and escaped to Egypt.

The wise men had been warned in a dream not to go back to Herod, and they returned to their own country by a different road.

After Herod's death, Jesus's family returned to Nazareth. When he was twelve, his parents took Jesus to the temple in Jerusalem for a festival. When it was over, Mary and Joseph set off home but didn't realize that Jesus wasn't with them. They went back and found him in the temple, asking the teachers questions. Everyone was amazed.

The years passed. A prophet, called John, told people to wash themselves in the River Jordan as a sign they wanted to lead a new life.

Jesus left his home in Nazareth and was baptized by John in the river. The spirit of God appeared like a dove, and a voice from heaven said, 'You are my dear son.'

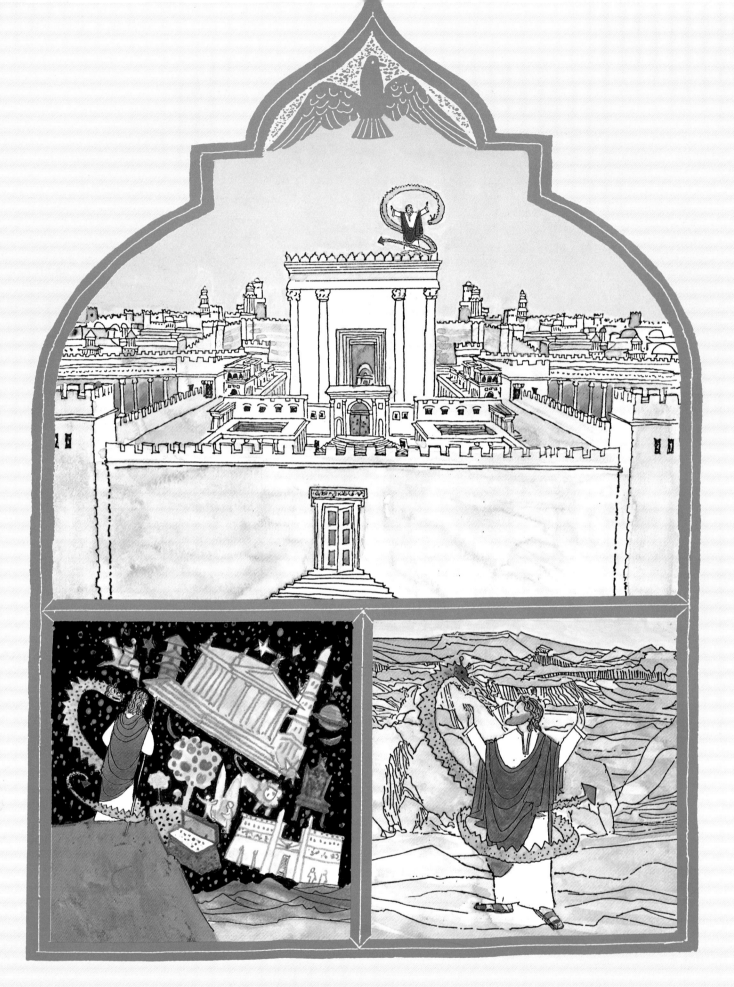

The Devil came to tempt Jesus in the desert. 'If you're hungry', said the Devil, 'turn these stones into bread.' But Jesus refused. The Devil then took him to the roof of the temple. 'Throw yourself down. God's angels will protect you', he said. Again Jesus refused.

He then showed Jesus all the kingdoms of the world and said, 'All this shall be yours if you worship me.' 'You should only worship God', said Jesus. And the Devil left him.

Jesus returned home and went with his mother to a wedding in Cana. The wine ran out before the party was over. 'Fill these jars with water', said Jesus. When the guests tasted it, the water had turned into very fine wine.

Later, Jesus was walking by the Sea of Galilee and saw Simon Peter and his brother Andrew fishing. 'Follow me and you will be fishers of men', said Jesus.

One day Jesus was out on Peter's fishing boat. 'Throw your net into the water,' he said. 'We've fished all night and caught nothing,' said Peter. But they did as Jesus had told them and the net came up full of fish.

Jesus went to a town called Nain. Near the city, bearers were carrying out a young man who had just died. He was his mother's only son, and she was a widow. Jesus said, 'Young man, rise up.' The dead man sat up and began to speak. And everyone was astonished.

Jesus then chose twelve special friends to be with him, and to help him with his work. He called them his disciples.

He sat down on the top of a hill and taught them, together with the crowds of people who had come to hear the Good News about God.

After supper Jesus and his friends went to the garden of Gethsemane. 'Sit here and keep watch while I pray', said Jesus. But his friends fell asleep, leaving Jesus alone.

'Father', Jesus prayed, 'save me from death. But only if that is what you want.'

Three times he prayed, and three times he went back to his friends. But they were still fast asleep.

Suddenly a crowd of people came into the garden, led by Judas, one of Jesus's friends.
They seized Jesus and dragged him to the house of Caiaphas, the chief priest.

'Are you the Son of God?' Caiaphas asked.

'I am', Jesus replied.

'You have all heard these terrible words', said Caiaphas. 'What do you say?'

'He deserves to die', they cried.

The priests took Jesus to Pilate, the Roman Governor, and accused him of many things.

'Have you no answer?' said Pilate. But Jesus did not reply.

'What shall I do with him?' asked Pilate.

'Crucify him!' they all shouted.

'Take him and crucify him then', said Pilate. 'I wash my hands of him'. So the soldiers gave Jesus a huge wooden cross and forced him to carry it.

They took Jesus to a hill outside the city.

There they crucified him between two thieves.

His friends placed the body of Jesus in a new tomb, cut out of the rock, and placed a heavy stone in front.

Early on Sunday two of Jesus's friends came. The stone had been rolled away and the body of Jesus was gone.

Two angels were there. 'He is not here,' said the angels. 'He is alive again.'

Near the tomb was a garden, and the women saw a man standing there. They thought he was the gardener, but when he turned round they knew it was Jesus.

'Don't be afraid', said Jesus. 'Run and tell all my friends to go up to Galilee, and they will see me there.'

Jesus's friends were so happy to see him again. He stayed with them for forty days, teaching them about the Kingdom of God.

But Jesus knew that it was near the time for him to leave this earth. As the sun rose one morning, he went up to his father in Heaven.

At the festival of Pentecost, the disciples were all together. Suddenly there was a sound as of a rushing wind and God's power touched them like flames of fire.

They went out into the world to tell people about Jesus and the Kingdom of God.

For Aurélie

OXFORD
UNIVERSITY PRESS

Great Clarendon Street, Oxford OX2 6DP

Oxford University Press is a department of the University of Oxford
It furthers the University's objective of excellence in research, scholarship,
and education by publishing worldwide in

Oxford New York

Athens Auckland Bangkok Bogotá Buenos Aires Cape Town
Chennai Dar es Salaam Delhi Florence Hong Kong Istanbul Karachi
Kolkata Kuala Lumpur Madrid Melbourne Mexico City Mumbai Nairobi
Paris São Paulo Shanghai Singapore Taipei Tokyo Toronto Warsaw

with associated companies in Berlin Ibadan

Oxford is a registered trade mark of Oxford University Press
in the UK and in certain other countries

First published 2000
Fist published in paperback 2002

British Library Cataloguing in
Publication Data available

ISBN 0 19 279059 5 HB
ISBN 0 19 272520 3 PB

Typeset by Mike Brain

1 3 5 7 9 10 8 6 4 2

Printed in Hong Kong

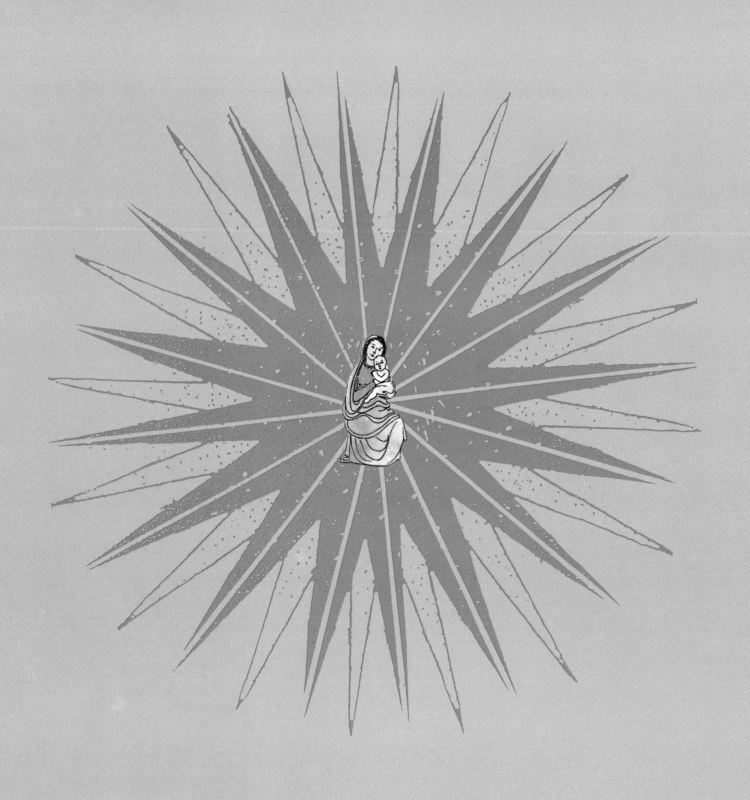